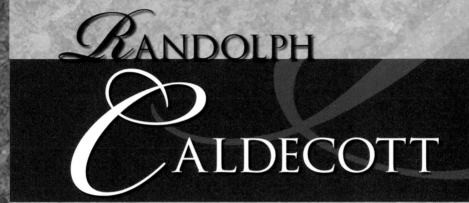

RANDOLPH CALDECOTT

Publishing Pioneers

RANDOLPH
CALDECOTT
RENOWNED BRITISH ILLUSTRATOR

by Rebecca Rowell

Content Consultant:
Gwen Patterson Reichert, EdM
Founder and Pres ____tt Society of America

ABDO
Publishing Company

CREDITS

Published by ABDO Publishing Company, 8000 West 78th Street, Edina, Minnesota 55439. Copyright © 2010 by Abdo Consulting Group, Inc. International copyrights reserved in all countries. No part of this book may be reproduced in any form without written permission from the publisher. The Essential Library™ is a trademark and logo of ABDO Publishing Company.

Printed in the United States.

 PRINTED ON RECYCLED PAPER

Editor: Paula Lewis
Copy Editor: Erika Wittekind
Interior Design and Production: Becky Daum
Cover Design: Becky Daum

Library of Congress Cataloging-in-Publication Data
Rowell, Rebecca.
  Randolph Caldecott : renowned British illustrator / by Rebecca Rowell.
     p. cm. — (Publishing pioneers)
  Includes bibliographical references and index.
  ISBN 978-1-60453-760-4
  1. Caldecott, Randolph, 1846-1886—Juvenile literature.
  2. Illustrators—England—Biography—Juvenile literature. I. Caldecott, Randolph, 1846-1886. II. Title. III. Title: Renowned British illustrator.
  NC978.5.C3R69 2009
  741.6'42092—dc22
  [B]
                                        2009009997

TABLE OF CONTENTS

Randolph Caldecott's illustration of a hunter

An Artist at Heart

It was a Monday, a Tuesday, or maybe a
Thursday. During the late 1860s, the days
often seemed the same at the Manchester & Salford
Bank. Customers entered the bank, took care of
their financial matters, and then departed. Every

day, clerks recorded entries, listing them in columns to tally. Some might find the predictability of working in a bank quite unappealing. Others—even those not truly bankers at heart—might find such an environment very attractive. Banks are ideal places to study people.

Randolph Caldecott was a young man working as a clerk at the renowned Manchester & Salford Bank in Manchester, England. Barely out of his teens, Caldecott had moved to Manchester in early 1867 to accept the position. This pleased his father, who was a successful businessman.

Born in a small English village, Caldecott had moved to Whitchurch in Shropshire, England, when he was 15 to work as a bank clerk. The move to Manchester was his second since leaving home. This opportunity would advance both his professional life and his personal life.

Manchester & Salford Bank

The Manchester & Salford Bank was established in 1836. The bank was first housed in a rented space on King Street in Manchester. The building Randolph Caldecott worked in as a clerk was located on Mosley Street. Designed by Edward Walters, the bank was built in 1862.

In 1890, Manchester & Salford acquired another bank, becoming Williams Deacon and Manchester & Salford Bank. In 1970, the bank became part of the Royal Bank of Scotland, which now occupies the Mosley location. From 1836 to 1970, the Manchester & Salford Bank opened almost 300 branches in England and Wales.

Victorian England

Born in 1846, Caldecott lived in Victorian England. The Victorian era (1837–1901) was the time during which Queen Victoria ruled Great Britain. Queen Victoria strove to regain and maintain Britain's political power. However, she also ended up making her role—and that of future monarchs—one of ceremony more than power.

The Victorian era was a time of great change in England. At the beginning of the 1800s, approximately 80 percent of the population lived in agricultural villages and rural areas. By the early 1900s, there had been a shift in population; 80 percent of the people lived in urban areas with factories and businesses. Reforms were passed that improved work and education, particularly for children. Nineteenth-century England has been described as an era "of strenuous activity and dynamic change, of ferment of ideas and recurrent social unrest, of great inventiveness and expansion."[1]

MANCHESTER

Manchester was one of England's wealthiest cities during the Victorian era. It was also the largest city Caldecott had lived in. Its size and wealth afforded Caldecott more opportunities than he had known in his young life. There was much for Caldecott to see and do when he was not behind his desk at Manchester & Salford. The library and a dozen local newspapers offered a variety of reading materials. Caldecott could visit the natural historical society or shop at Manchester's busy and active market. To meet people and make new friends, he could join one of many clubs for businessmen or simply stop by a local pub.

But there was never quite enough time for such activities. Just as thousands of others in England did, Caldecott spent most of his days working. The bank training he received in Whitchurch appeared to

The Industrial Revolution brought train service between Manchester and London.

make the young man a good fit for his new position at Manchester & Salford. Seated at one of the bank's many desks, Caldecott was surrounded by the ornate decor of the plaster ceiling and gold-tipped columns. He seemed to succeed in his new position. He completed his work and took pride in it. He also got along well with the other employees, especially William Clough, who became a lifelong friend.

Caldecott brought to his work the good nature and kindness he presented in the other areas of his life. He had a good sense of humor and even became known as a joker.

Yet, in other ways, Caldecott was serious. He carefully observed everything around him. He had always been this way. As a young boy, Caldecott enjoyed the English countryside where he lived. He studied nature and expressed what he saw artistically. Using wood, clay, and paint, he recreated the animals that he observed near his home.

Manchester, England

The site of present-day Manchester, England, was initially a Roman fort built between the years 76 and 86. In the early third century, the fort was rebuilt. After being unoccupied for approximately 500 years, King Edward the Elder ordered it repaired in 919 to defend against Norse raiders. By this time, people had begun settling near the site at a location where two rivers met.

A charter establishing Manchester as a town was granted in 1301. A grammar school was established in the early 1500s. By this time, the town had a booming wool trade. The cotton industry grew in the following century.

The Industrial Revolution brought growth and change to Manchester. The first canal opened in 1762, bringing Manchester new importing and exporting opportunities. The city's first cotton mill was established during the 1780s. The Liverpool and Manchester Railway was the first modern railway. It opened in 1830 and, within 20 years, it linked to other lines throughout Great Britain.

Eventually, Manchester became a center for commerce and finance more than for cotton manufacturing. By the Victorian era, when Caldecott lived there, Manchester had become an exciting city that had grown in terms of population, politics, and culture.

Caldecott's desire to record the world around him in artistic ways carried into adulthood. He continued to sketch images of the nature and wildlife he had always enjoyed. At work, he studied people. His desk in the bank's great hall was an ideal spot for viewing all the comings and goings at Manchester & Salford. He approached his work at the bank—and the many patrons who visited each day—just as he did everything else. Caldecott enjoyed life: living it, studying it, and capturing it in ink on paper or through other mediums. Quickly, he sketched customers, as well as his coworkers, on scraps of paper. His sketches might combine many different elements on the page. One of his sketches was described as a mix of various drawings:

> [A] gentleman in stove-pipe trousers and tall hat was placed next to a donkey's head; sheets of portrait heads on envelope edges recorded elements of character; a miserly-looking old man . . . landscapes . . . drawn with a delicate etcher's line.[2]

CHOOSING AN ARTISTIC LIFE

Manchester was a good location for Caldecott. In addition to being a place where he earned a living, the vibrant city with a growing population provided ample opportunities to observe life. Caldecott could draw whatever suited him—people, buildings, public celebrations, and events. With a trip to the nearby countryside, he could continue to explore, enjoy, and sketch the nature he so loved.

But Manchester offered more than work and subjects for Caldecott to draw. The city was home to the Manchester School of Art, where he was enrolled. The Brasenose Club proved to be an important social organization for Caldecott and other young men. His membership connected him with other artists and art lovers. Art was what Caldecott enjoyed and aspired to do for a living.

Caldecott lived in Manchester for five years, working, observing, recording, and learning. During this time, he made an important decision: art would be his profession. Within years of choosing art over banking, Randolph Caldecott would become a household name in England. His creations would be viewed well beyond the borders of England. Countless readers worldwide would see and appreciate Caldecott's gifts—during his lifetime and well into the future.

A colored version of Randolph Caldecott's 1875 illustration of a Christmas feast

Chapter 2

Chester, England

YOUNG RANDOLPH

John Caldecott and Mary Dinah Brookes married in September 1842. The young English couple's first child, John, was born the following summer. Their second son, William, was born in August 1844. Randolph was the couple's third child. He was born in the family's home in Chester, England, on March 22, 1846.

John Caldecott was a businessman who worked in Chester. Trained as an accountant, he owned his own wool shop in the Rows, Chester's busy marketplace on Bridge Street. He made drapes, hats, and clothes. Above the shop, where the family lived, Mary Caldecott cared for their children.

The Caldecotts lived on Bridge Street until Randolph was a toddler. Perhaps because the family was still growing, a larger space was needed. In 1848, the little boy with curly brown hair and gray-blue eyes moved with his family to Challoner House on Crook Street in Chester. This would be the first of many moves Randolph would make throughout his life. For now, he would explore and become familiar with Chester and its natural surroundings. It was the beginning of a lifetime appreciation for nature and wildlife.

The Caldecott Children

In many countries and cultures, children have a first and a middle name. Generally, this is not the case in England. As a result, Randolph Caldecott and his younger siblings do not have middle names.

John and Mary Caldecott had seven children:
- John George (1843–1879)
- William Brookes (1844–1846)
- Randolph (1846–1886)
- Sophia (1848–1929)
- Elizabeth (1849–1850)
- Alfred (1850–1941)
- Harold (1852–1871)

Mary Caldecott, Randolph's mother, died on August 21, 1852. John Caldecott remarried in 1854. He and his second wife, Maria, had six children.

The Artist Emerges

Chester is in Cheshire County. The city is located approximately 170 miles (275 km) northwest of London, in England's countryside, on the Dee River. Founded in the year 85 by Romans, the city's population neared 30,000 by the mid-1800s. Chester was still surrounded by the wall the Romans had built centuries before Caldecott's birth.

Randolph often roamed beyond Chester's ancient Roman wall to the nearby countryside. He walked the area, taking in the many sights and sounds that surrounded him. Playful squirrels scampered about, chasing one another around trees. Tentative rabbits hopped and then stood still at the slightest sound or movement to observe the area. Beautiful birds chirped, sang, and flitted from tree to tree.

Randolph recorded his many observations in sketchbooks. He also expressed himself—and the nature and wildlife he investigated—in other forms. As a young boy of only six, he painted, modeled clay, and carved animals from wood.

Randolph was not always well. He suffered from rheumatic fever when he was a young boy. This illness gave him fevers, made his joints swollen and painful, and weakened his heart. Randolph became prone to illness, but his poor health was not constant.

When he was old enough, Randolph attended the King's School in Chester. The school had been founded in 1541 by King Henry VIII and was located next to Chester Cathedral. Classes were taught in the monastery's refectory, or dining hall. The school had fewer than 20 students. While he was a student at King's School, Randolph was not the most studious pupil. He did enjoy art, though he drew in a place

Chester, England

The English village of Randolph's birth, Chester, was founded by Romans in the year 85. They called the location *Deva* or *Castra Devana*. The Romans built a wall around Chester that still stands today and is a landmark of the city. Other Roman structures remain, including an amphitheater.

Chester received its city charter in 1176. By that time, the city was trading with Wales and Ireland. Chester became a valued stop on the River Dee for boats during the thirteenth and fourteenth centuries. Trade with Ireland was particularly strong. As with Manchester, the creation of British railways breathed new life into Chester during the 1800s. At that time, the city thrived.

Chester is known for the Rows. This is a shopping area of two-tiered buildings where the upper level juts out over the lower level. Chester Cathedral is another landmark. Its history is centuries long. The church was founded in 660, and a monastery was founded in 1092. The monastery was dissolved in 1539, but King Henry VIII established the Diocese of Chester on July 26, 1541. As the seat of the diocese, the church became Chester Cathedral.

Midday proclamations are another interesting city attraction. Each day, town criers proclaim public announcements. The practice has been in place since the 1500s.

Chester Bridge

his teachers likely would not have approved—his schoolbooks.

Years later, Arthur Locker, a newspaper editor, wrote of Randolph:

> *He must have begun . . . at a very early age, for just after Caldecott's death, the writer of these lines picked up at a bookstall a ragged old Virgil which had belonged to [Caldecott] when a Chester schoolboy, and which was adorned with sundry [various] pen and ink sketches, exhibiting, however it must be frankly said, no more special talent than is shown by scores of lads who have a turn for drawing. . . . It was only gradually that Caldecott discovered his real vocation.*[1]

SETTING OUT ON HIS OWN

In 1861, Randolph decided to leave school. He was 15 years old and ready to strike out on his own. Randolph left Chester for Whitchurch, located in the county of Shropshire. He moved approximately 25 miles (40 km) southeast of his family's home. The town was named for a white church that had once stood there. Whitchurch was a fraction of the size of Chester. But Randolph found work as a clerk at the Whitchurch & Ellesmere Bank. As a businessman, John Caldecott thought his son should pursue serious endeavors. A bank clerk was a respectable position. It met the approval of Randolph's father, who had discouraged his son's early artistic endeavors.

Though he worked in Whitchurch, Randolph did not live in the town. Instead, he took up residence approximately two miles (3 km) outside of Whitchurch. He lived in an old farmhouse in the countryside.

Randolph took advantage of this home in the country. Just as he had done as a young boy in Chester, the teenager wandered the area and drew what he saw. He participated in other outdoor activities as well, including fishing and hunting.

Not all of Randolph's pursuits were solitary. He was outgoing and enjoyed being around people, so he would visit friends and plan parties. He also frequented markets and cattle fairs.

Randolph did well in Whitchurch. In addition to his job at the bank, he took up work for the bank as an insurance agent. Work for the Whitchurch & Ellesmere Bank was not always conducted in the office. Transactions were often completed at customers' farms or town halls.

Attending to tasks outside the office allowed Randolph to become acquainted with his new surroundings and enjoy the outdoors. Randolph's kind nature made him well liked by both coworkers and customers. A friend noted the following about Randolph:

> The young lad carried his own recommendation. With light brown hair falling with a ripple over his brow, blue–

Selling Life Insurance

Randolph's additional work as a life insurance agent was not successful. James M. Etches, a friend, wrote about one of Randolph's experiences. Caldecott had not made a sale, but one farmer was somewhat interested in life insurance. However, the farmer mistakenly believed that he would receive the money if he were still alive in one year. Randolph explained that the farmer's beneficiary would receive the money if the farmer died within the year. The farmer decided against buying the policy and walked out of the bank "leaving an open-mouthed young Caldecott standing at the counter."[2]

grey eyes shaded by long lashes, sweet and mobile mouth, tall and well made, he joined to these physical advantages a gay humour and a charming disposition.[3]

Randolph experienced many firsts while living in Whitchurch. He was living on his own for the first time. He was working at his first job. And he was published for the first time when one of his drawings appeared in a newspaper. The drawing was of the Queen Railway Hotel, which had been built in Chester in 1860. In November 1861, it caught fire. Randolph happened to witness the catastrophe. His love of drawing prompted the aspiring artist to always have paper and pencil at hand. As flames and smoke engulfed the building, survivors bolted from it and gathered with the growing number of onlookers. Surrounded by chaos, Randolph kept a steady hand and, as

Whitchurch, England

Whitchurch was founded by the Romans in 70. They named the town *Mediolanum*, Latin for "the place in the mid-plain." The site was chosen for its location on a key route between *Deva* (present-day Chester) and *Viroconium* (present-day Wroxeter).

Unlike other Roman-founded English cities, Whitchurch has few remnants of Roman occupation. However, relics from other eras have been found nearby.

Whitchurch is known for its tower clocks. Clockmaker JB Joyce & Co. was founded in 1690 and moved to Whitchurch in 1834. Known as Smith of Derby since 1965, the company is the world's oldest manufacturer of tower clocks.

was his way, captured the event on paper. Randolph's detailed depiction was published in the *Illustrated London News* on December 7, 1861. He was 15 years old.

In late 1861, all was going well for young Randolph. He loved nature and art. He had been published and learned that he could make money drawing. And though he did well in Whitchurch, by 1866, the 20-year-old aspiring artist was ready for change. On Christmas Eve of that year, he had a meeting that would result in yet another move. Manchester was Randolph's next destination.

Romans built walls around the city of Chester.

Manchester was home to textile industries, including cotton and wool.

MANCHESTER

In late 1866, 20-year-old Randolph Caldecott decided it was time for something different. He had been in Whitchurch for more than five years and was ready for change. On December 24, as others prepared for and celebrated Christmas in England, Caldecott met with William Langton about a job. Langton was the managing director of the Manchester & Salford Bank in Manchester, England. Part of his job was hiring employees, and he offered Caldecott a position.

ANOTHER MOVE

Caldecott accepted Langton's offer to work as a clerk at the bank. This change in employment meant Caldecott would move again. But he did not mind; this was a move that he sought.

Caldecott settled in Manchester in 1867. The city is located approximately 36 miles (58 km) northeast of Chester in the county of Lancashire. As a center for textile production in the county, the city was wealthy. It also had a large population. With more than 400,000 residents in the mid-1800s, Manchester was considerably larger than Chester and Whitchurch. Given the size of the city and its population, Manchester boasted a variety of new places for Caldecott to explore and new people to meet. Manchester was an appropriate place for Caldecott. The city broadened his horizons. It simply had more to offer than his small hometown and Whitchurch.

City of Libraries

One of Manchester's claims to fame is its libraries. The city is home to Chetham Library, Britain's first free public library. Founded in 1653, it is the oldest library in the English-speaking world.

Humphrey Chetham left money to buy books for his proposed scholarly library and to create other libraries in Manchester.

The building was also a charitable hospital, which meant it provided free education to young boys from poor families. The idea of a free public library was new to England.

Today, the charitable hospital is a school for musically gifted young men and women. Admission to the school is based on talent; scholarships are awarded to those with financial hardships.

Just as he had done as a young boy in Chester and a young man in Whitchurch, Caldecott explored his surroundings. He not only familiarized himself with Manchester, Caldecott also visited the surrounding countryside. As had been his habit since childhood, Caldecott continued to record his observations on paper in sketches and illustrations. Caldecott continually worked on his skills as an artist. This included drawing while at work.

Manchester & Salford was more demanding than Whitchurch & Ellesmere. Although his job in Manchester required more of his time and attention than his job in Whitchurch, Caldecott still found time to draw. People of all ages, sizes, and backgrounds took care of their financial business at the bank. Sitting behind his large wooden desk in the bank's beautiful hall, Caldecott sketched the many characters who passed by each day, including his coworkers. He scribbled in pencil

Chetham's Library (shown in 1937) was built in the seventeenth century.

on stationery and envelopes or any bits of paper at hand. Coworkers' faces were drawn on scraps from the bank—sometimes next to calculations.

William Clough worked with Caldecott at Manchester & Salford. The two became friends. Clough wrote of Caldecott:

> *Caldecott used to wander about the bustling, murky streets of Manchester, sometimes finding himself in queer out-of-the-way quarters often coming across an odd character, curious bits of antiquity and the like. Whenever the chance came he made short excursions into the adjacent country,*

and long walks which were never purposeless. . . . Whilst in this city so close was his application to the art that he loved that on several occasions he spent the whole night drawing.[1]

ART STUDENT AND ART LOVER

Manchester presented Caldecott with an assortment of new opportunities. He could learn about past and present topics at the city's libraries and in its many newspapers. He could also explore and develop his creative side at the Manchester School of Art. He became a student, taking classes in the evening. Though he was a student at the art school for only a short time, his artistic endeavors continued. He continued to work on his artistic skills on his own. He always practiced, taking advantage of wherever he was to observe and draw.

Not a Banker

In 1885, Caldecott wrote to William Clough about a banking associate who had died, "As for me, I am sure I must have caused him moments of dissatisfaction and uneasiness. There was seldom visible in me any steady sober respect for the work of the bank."[2]

As Caldecott got to know Manchester and all it had to offer, the aspiring artist met and befriended other artists. Clubs were popular at the time, so there were several he could join. Caldecott became a member of the Brasenose Club, an association for businessmen. Brasenose strove "to promote the association of gentlemen of literary, scientific, or artistic professions, pursuits or tastes."[3] Club members consisted of men who worked in a variety of professions, including actors, artists, journalists, and poets. The time Caldecott spent at the Brasenose Club provided invaluable networking opportunities. He participated in the club's activities and socialized with its members.

Finally, he was surrounded by like-minded individuals. Some members were in the position Caldecott aspired to be in— professional artist. He could learn

The Brasenose Club

When Randolph Caldecott joined the Brasenose Club, it had not been in existence for very long. Created in 1869, the club wanted "to promote the association of gentlemen of Literary, Scientific or Artistic Professions, Pursuits or Tastes."[4] The club's name came from its location on Brazennose Street. The club moved to a new address, on Mosley Street, in 1892. The new location had been built for the National and Provincial Bank. It would be home to the Brasenose Club for 41 years.

During the Victorian era, and shortly thereafter, clubs were popular in Manchester. Such clubs provided a welcoming environment to men, particularly young men such as Caldecott, who had recently moved to the city. For an aspiring artist, the Brasenose Club provided Caldecott and other young artists "exceptional opportunities of seeing good work, and obtaining information on art matters."[5]

But clubs such as the Brasenose lost their popularity. This was particularly so in the 1930s. In January 1933, members of the Brasenose Club transferred their memberships to the Clarendon Club. The Brasenose Club closed. In 1962, Clarendon merged with Union Club and formed the St. James Club.

from other members' knowledge and experience. He was in good company.

As he spent more and more time drawing, those who knew Caldecott could see his talent. A coworker at Manchester & Salford wrote of his dear friend's lack of impressiveness as a bank clerk:

> *Caldecott's ability was general, not special. It found its natural and most agreeable outlet in art and humour, but everybody who knew him, and those who received his letters, saw that there were perhaps a dozen ways in which he would have distinguished himself had he been drawn to them.*[6]

A Good Clerk

Although Randolph Caldecott was an artist at heart who spent time drawing at work, he also completed the tasks he was assigned. The records of Caldecott's employment at the Manchester & Salford Bank show that the young clerk did his job well.

While in Manchester, Caldecott got a taste of what it was like to be a professional artist. Some of his drawings were published in two local papers: the *Will o' the Wisp* and the *Sphinx*. The artwork was amateurish, which reflected the young artist's mostly self-taught skills. Caldecott also exhibited his first painting in the city. In 1869, *At the Wrong End of the Wood*, a hunting painting, was displayed at the Royal Manchester Institution.

LONDON CALLS

The following year, 1870, would present new opportunities to Caldecott. London was a hub for many things during the Victorian era. As England's capital, the busy city was home to many banks, schools, and businesses. But it was more than a place for finance, education, and commerce. London was also a center for the arts. Not surprisingly, Caldecott was drawn to the bustling city. In May of that year, Caldecott visited London. He introduced himself to Thomas Armstrong, an accomplished painter and designer. Caldecott showed Armstrong some samples of his work that he had brought to London.

The meeting with Armstrong went well and marked the beginning of a friendship in which Armstrong would mentor Caldecott. After Caldecott's visit to London, Armstrong shared some of the aspiring artist's work with Henry Blackburn, the editor of the magazine *London Society.* On November 30, 1870, Caldecott wrote in his diary:

> *Some drawings which I left with [Armstrong] in London have been shown, accompanied by a letter from du Maurier, to a man on* London Society. *Must wait a bit and go on working—especially studying horses, [Armstrong] said.* [7]

Only two months later, in February 1871, Caldecott's work was published for the first time in *London Society*. He now had a new, larger audience—London. He continued to send Blackburn illustrations, many of which were published. Caldecott submitted so many drawings in various styles and on numerous topics that Blackburn wrote in 1871, "What to do with all the material sent?"[8]

With his drawings printed in almost every issue of *London Society*, Caldecott was making a name for himself in London. He also received praise from critics who enjoyed his humorous renderings in the periodical. Even with this success, Caldecott continued to work in other mediums. In early 1872, Caldecott sold two paintings: one done in oil and the other in watercolor. The successes in London and Manchester prompted Caldecott to make a bold decision. After five years in Manchester, it was time to pursue his dream on a full-time basis. But first, he would have to move once more. London was calling the 26-year-old artist.

Lack of Encouragement

When Caldecott was young, his father discouraged him from pursuing art. As Caldecott traveled farther from home, he met more people who were artists or interested in the arts. The aspiring artist finally received the support his father had not offered.

Manchester in the nineteenth century

A busy London street in 1872

LONDON

The early 1870s had been productive and positive for Randolph Caldecott. He had visited London and made important connections with artist Thomas Armstrong and editor Henry Blackburn. His drawings began to be published regularly in a London magazine, and two of his paintings were sold in Manchester. Caldecott was succeeding as an artist. He decided it was time to turn to art for his career.

When Caldecott quit his job as a clerk at the Manchester & Salford Bank in early 1872, he did not have a position waiting for him in London. He was not moving to accept a job at another bank. Rather, he was moving to London to pursue his passion. Caldecott decided to make art more than a hobby:

> *I had the money in my pocket sufficient to keep me for a year or so, and was hopeful that during that time my powers would be developed and my style improved so much that I should find plenty of work.*[1]

THE CITY

The 185 miles (298 km) from Manchester to London would bring a world of change to Caldecott—especially from the rural life he had experienced as a youth. And while Manchester was a well-to-do and growing city, it was considerably smaller than England's capital city. In 1872, London was a metropolis with more than 3 million inhabitants.

London was a city of extremes. There were wealthy, successful people and businesses. Impressive buildings were being designed and erected, and the city was growing. On the other hand, the Industrial Revolution and the Irish Potato Famine had brought many people to London to seek their fortune and refuge. Many of these people had little money and ended up living in overcrowded slums with terrible conditions. The city was dirty, noisy, and crowded. It was very different from the rural landscapes Caldecott had grown up in.

And although the city had many more people than Chester, Whitchurch, and Manchester combined, Caldecott was alone. He no longer saw his pals at the bank every day. He worked alone. He lived alone. As a newcomer to London, he had not yet established the strong friendships he was accustomed to enjoying. But this would soon change.

Population Boom

The city of London experienced tremendous growth during the 1800s. At the beginning of the century, its population was just under 1 million. By the end of the century, the city had grown to more than 4 million people.

The rapid increase of inhabitants was due to the Industrial Revolution, which improved and increased travel. It also introduced jobs that brought workers from the rural areas. In addition, more than 100,000 Irish immigrants settled in London to escape the potato famine in their homeland and seek a better life.

Caldecott lived across from the British Museum.

SETTLING IN

Caldecott moved to 46 Great Russell Street. His apartment was across from the British Museum. This served him well as an excellent location for an aspiring artist. Once settled in, he began to explore his new surroundings. As Caldecott wandered the streets to take in London's many sights and sounds, he undoubtedly encountered a wealth of subjects to observe and draw.

A journalist wrote of Caldecott:

He would stroll down to the Houses of Parliament and sketch the members . . . . If there was a fashionable wedding, a meeting at Exeter Hall, a great public gathering of any kind, a new piece at the theatre, he made one of the party. He frequented the Parks and roamed about the streets . . . neither pencil nor imagination was ever at rest. [2]

After moving to London, Caldecott continued to draw for the *London Society*. Although the young man had many supporters, his art was not always well received by everyone:

The sketches were made always from his own point of view, and some were so grotesque, and hit so hard at aristocracy, that they were found inappropriate to a fashionable magazine! [3]

Blackburn ignored such criticism. He continued to encourage and support Caldecott—as an editor and as a friend.

Criticism

Although Caldecott's work was popular with many, it did not always receive good reviews. A reader of *London Society* wrote a letter to the magazine in 1872 stating that the artist could not draw a lady. In response, Caldecott drew a sketch of himself in front of an easel. His back is to the viewer. A lovely woman is seated to Caldecott's right. She is facing away from him, posing. He is busy faithfully creating her image in ink.

Caldecott contributed regularly to *London Society* and other publications of the large city. As he made drawings, Caldecott continued to work on his craft. While becoming increasingly adept at sketching scenes, he began creating cartoonlike drawings that exaggerated a quality or trait of his subject. To develop his artistic skills, he painted wildlife. Caldecott also trained in art. From April 16 to June 29, 1872, he studied art at the Slade School.

CONNECTIONS

Caldecott networked as well. He made new

Thomas Armstrong

Thomas Armstrong was born on October 19, 1832, in Manchester, England. His first career path was in business, but that was short-lived. As a young man, Armstrong moved to Paris, France, where he became a student of Ary Scheffer, a Dutch painter and sculptor. Armstrong lived in and traveled throughout Europe and northern Africa for a few years practicing his painting. He moved to London around 1860.

Armstrong's style changed during his career. Initially, he painted images with social themes. After a few years, his style became more classical and decorative and less focused on telling a story. After approximately ten years of working in this style, Armstrong focused on painting landscapes and portraits.

In addition to being an artist, Armstrong held the position of director of the art division of the Department of Science and Art at the South Kensington Museum from 1881 to 1898. In this role, he organized art education in Britain. He also worked in acquisitions, obtaining art for the museum.

Armstrong was also a husband and father. He married Alice Brine in 1881. The couple had a son, Ambrose, who died in 1894 at the age of 11. Thomas Armstrong died on April 22, 1911. He was 78 years old.

acquaintances and formed a circle of friends who appreciated, encouraged, and supported his artistic talents. Many of his friends were artists and men in publishing. E. J. Poynter was known for his epic paintings. He also was an illustrator and created designs for stained glass and decorative furniture. Poynter was Caldecott's art professor at the Slade School. James Whistler was a painter from the United States. Charles Keene was a comic illustrator. George du Maurier was a writer and illustrator. Caldecott met Jules Dalou as well. The French sculptor instructed Caldecott in clay modeling in exchange for English lessons.

Perhaps the most notable of Caldecott's many connections in London was the one he had with Thomas Armstrong, the artist he had traveled to London to meet in 1870. The meeting was the beginning of a lifelong relationship. Armstrong

Editor, Publisher, Author

When Caldecott met him, Henry Blackburn was the editor of the monthly magazine *London Society*. Blackburn dabbled in several areas of publishing. In addition to being an editor, he was also a publisher and a writer. Blackburn wrote books about places and people. His biography of Caldecott, *Randolph Caldecott: A Personal Memoir of his Early Art Career*, was published in 1890.

Cartoon in Punch *by artist Charles Keene*

would become Caldecott's best friend and his mentor. The two men met regularly. Armstrong provided guidance for what the young artist should practice. Sometimes it was drawing caricatures, while other times it was modeling with wax or painting birds. He also gave Caldecott work and a space in which to do it.

Starving Artist

Although his work was published regularly, Randolph Caldecott was likely in need of money while becoming professionally established. In 1872, the new editor of *London Society* contacted Caldecott about creating a series of drawings for a novelette that would be published in a series of issues of the magazine. Caldecott expressed interest in the project, writing to a friend, "I think I shall do them, I want coin!"[4]

Caldecott's move to London in 1872 and transition from working as a bank clerk to working as an artist went smoothly. He settled in and explored the city, always observing and recording his surroundings and the people in his sketches and drawings. He made important professional and personal connections that led to paying work as an artist. His career as an artist was off to a good start. More projects were on the horizon that would further Caldecott's career and bring him new successes.

LIVELY APPEARANCE OF REGENT STREET IN JUNE.

...ERFAMILIAS TAKES HIS FAMILY TO THE SEA-SIDE CHEAPLY.

OLD LADY CAUGHT BY THE WEST WIND AND BLOWN CITYWA...

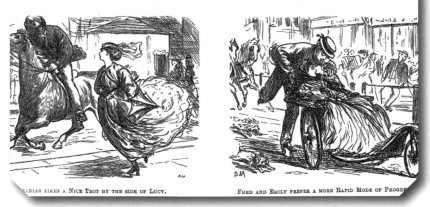

...HARLES LIKES A NICE TROT BY THE SIDE OF LUCY.

FRED AND EMILY PREFER A MORE RAPID MODE OF PROGRE...

Cartoon in Punch *by George du Maurier*

E. J. Poynter

SUCCESS!

Randolph Caldecott's move to London to work as an artist had been a good decision. He met many talented and important people in the art and publishing worlds who would help him further his skills and his career.

The summer of 1872 was a busy one for the young artist. In addition to studying under E. J. Poynter at the Slade School, Caldecott's work was published in another London periodical. He had submitted several drawings to *Punch*, a humor magazine. His first piece was published on June 22, 1872.

Caldecott also exhibited some of his artwork that month. Four small sepia drawings were put on display in London's Egyptian Hall as part of the annual Black and White Exhibition. The summer would also bring the young man his first commission, or contracted, work.

First Commission

Only months after deciding to pursue art as a profession, Caldecott was well on his way. His developing London relationships and his devotion to illustrating were important to his success. Henry Blackburn was the editor of *London Society* and had a reputation among

London Society

London Society was published from February 1862 to December 1898. During that time, the monthly magazine had five publishers and printed 441 issues. Content consisted of poetry, sketches, and short stories—including ghost and horror tales. *London Society* advertised itself as "an illustrated magazine of light and amusing literature for the hours of relaxation."[1]

artists for being difficult to work with. However, he regularly published Caldecott's drawings. He also encouraged the young artist to pursue the art of illustration. Blackburn further promoted Caldecott's craft by offering the illustrator his first commissioned book in the summer of 1872. Caldecott accepted.

In August, the 26-year-old joined the Blackburns on a trip to the Netherlands and Germany. In addition to being an editor, Blackburn was a travel writer.

Sketching People

Caldecott paid close attention to his surroundings. He wrote about sketching people and included sketches of people in his correspondence. In a letter to Whitchurch friend William Baker Etches, dated March 29, 1873, Caldecott wrote:

I enjoyed the sight of the many thousands of people; it was good fun to watch the manner of passing away the time before the race. This was about the best.

I noticed one young creature busily engaged in sketching the people. I mentally sketched. Here she is—and the man she was sketching.[2]

The artist often included himself in his drawings. *Spectres of the Brocken* is one of the illustrations Caldecott created for Blackburn's book *The Harz Mountains: A Tour in the Toy Country*. The drawing depicts a half dozen people out in the dark, cold, and rain of the Harz Mountains. Some carry umbrellas. The characters are shown from behind. Five of them are average size or larger. The sixth person, standing on the left, is tall and thin. His scarf is blowing in the wind, and his hands are in his pockets. It is Caldecott.

At times, the artist concentrated on a single human feature. His first small sketchbook in London includes a page of only feet in shoes.

He and his wife were taking the trip so he could gather research for a book, which Caldecott would illustrate.

The Harz Mountains: A Tour in the Toy Country was published in 1873. It included two dozen drawings by Caldecott. The images ranged from a dance of witches to landscapes to natives conducting daily life.

Caldecott received a second book commission in early 1873. He drew six illustrations for *The Naval Officer or Scenes and Adventures in the Life of Frank Mildmay.* Blackburn continued to help Caldecott build his career as an artist. During a trip to New York that year to promote his book, Blackburn shared some of Caldecott's work with a U.S. magazine. In June 1873, *Harper's New Monthly Magazine* published 22 of Caldecott's drawings as part of an 18-page excerpt from Blackburn's book about the Harz Mountains.

Three months later, Caldecott's work would appear in a different New York publication. He had attended the Vienna International Exhibition in Austria. Blackburn arranged for Caldecott's drawings of the event to be printed in the *New York Daily Graphic.* Caldecott now not only had a new source of income, he also had a new audience in the United States.

Pieces of Caldecott's art were exhibited in London's Egyptian Hall.

PAINTER

Caldecott's move to London brought him work and recognition as an illustrator. This success did not focus the artist's attention solely on illustration. He continued to pursue his other artistic interests. Caldecott had studied painting in Manchester and continued to paint after moving to London under the encouragement of Thomas Armstrong. Painting was a means for Caldecott to practice and expand his skills as an artist.

It also provided Caldecott another means for earning an income. Armstrong designed interiors for buildings in and around London. He gave Caldecott professional painting work on some of his design commissions. For example, Caldecott created birds for Armstrong in one project. In April 1874, Caldecott wrote in his diary that he had drawn and painted storks, swans, pigeons, and magpies. Sometimes, Caldecott's work appeared on walls. Sometimes, it was on furniture. In 1874, Caldecott worked with Armstrong on panels six feet (1.8 m) high as part of a project at Bank Hall in Chapel-en-le-Frith, Derbyshire. The men were decorating a dining room in the home of Henry Renshaw. The panels Caldecott and Armstrong created for Bank Hall were exhibited in a gallery that same year.

MORE NEWSPAPER WORK

Caldecott's career had taken off and was going well. It had even expanded to a new continent: North America. Although his work was

A Letter Writer

No matter how busy he was, Randolph Caldecott always took time to correspond with his friends and acquaintances. He was a devoted letter writer. After moving to London, Caldecott continued his friendship with William Clough, his coworker at Manchester & Salford. The two would exchange letters regularly. In addition to sharing news from his life or addressing other matters, Caldecott often drew in his letters.

advancing, Caldecott's health was not. It sometimes proved challenging. The rheumatic fever he had suffered as a child left Caldecott with health issues as an adult. In March 1873, he wrote:

> *About the middle of February I went down into the country to make some studies and sketches, and remained for more than a month. Had several smart attacks on the heart, a little wounded once.*[3]

However, Caldecott's poor health did not keep him from doing his work or acquiring new projects. The young artist continued to illustrate for the *London Society* and the book commissions. Caldecott acquired other clients as well. In mid-1873, the 27-year-old began working as a special reporter for two newspapers: the *Graphic* in London and the *Daily Graphic* in New York.

Although the newspaper work was welcome, it was also long and tiring. This was especially so for Caldecott because of his health. Harry Furniss was a special reporter who drew for *Illustrated London News*, another London newspaper. He wrote of the role:

> *I sat up all night and drew a page on wood, ready for engraving, and sent it off by the first train in the morning. It was in the press before my rival's rough notes left Liverpool.*

This cartoon by Harry Furniss depicts the 1885 meeting of
the Zoological Society in London.

. . . *All day again sketching, and all night hard at work,*
burning the midnight oil (I was nearly writing books). . . .
And after another day of this kind of thing, I reached home
without having had an hour's sleep. Oh! A "special's" life is
not a happy one. [4]

The fast pace of the newspaper industry proved
to be too much for Caldecott. He could not manage

Harz Mountains

In August 1872, Caldecott traveled to the Harz Mountains with the Blackburns. The Harz Mountains are the northernmost mountain range in Germany. The range is 56 miles (90 km) long and 19 miles (31 km) wide. Brockenberg is one of the Harz's peaks. It is said that witches and goblins frequent Brockenberg.

the work of special reporter on a regular basis. It was too tiring and demanding.

But Caldecott would not be without income. In 1874, Henry Blackburn took a new position that would bring work to Caldecott. Other opportunities would arise as well. Caldecott would soon form a partnership and begin a project that would take his career in a new direction.

Caldecott traveled in the Harz Mountains with Blackburn.

Washington Irving

A NEW DIRECTION

By the end of 1873, 27-year-old Randolph Caldecott had experienced success as a professional artist. His illustrations had been published at home and abroad, and he had received his first commissions.

Caldecott's career continued to advance in 1874. In addition to doing more work with Blackburn, Caldecott began a new business relationship with James D. Cooper, an accomplished engraver. The work of an engraver was an art in its own right. Cooper would engrave, or cut, the artist's drawings into woodblocks by cutting away all of the white areas. The remaining ridges on the block were inked, and the block was used to print the lines in the original drawing onto paper.

Three years earlier, Cooper had worked on the artist's first published illustration, *A Debating Society*, which appeared in *London Society*. In his diary for January 23, 1874, the artist wrote:

> *J. Cooper . . . proposed to illustrate with seventy or eighty sketches, Washington Irving's* Sketch Book. *Went all through it and left me to consider. I like the idea.*[1]

Not only did Caldecott like Cooper's idea, he pursued it. He and Cooper formed a partnership that would take the artist's career in a new direction.

Old Christmas

When Cooper visited Caldecott on January 23, he left a copy of Washington Irving's *The Sketch Book of Geoffrey Crayon*. Published in 1820, Irving's book was a collection of essays and short stories set in England from 1805 to 1815. There were no drawings or illustrations. Cooper wanted Caldecott to create images for Irving's book. Caldecott was excited about the project and promptly began interpreting the text pictorially.

Based on parts of Irving's sketch book, *Old Christmas* would be a book about celebrating Christmas in an English manor house. Caldecott would draw upon his years of observation and practice to bring Irving's words about the topic to life in drawings. Chester, Whitchurch, the English countryside, and many other places Caldecott had seen would find their way onto the pages of *Old Christmas*. This was an ideal project for the artist.

Caldecott spent the summer of 1874 illustrating *Old Christmas*. Cooper spent much of the following year engraving the artist's illustrations. *Old Christmas* came out in October 1875. The book included five chapters from Irving's original work, and Caldecott contributed 120 illustrations.

Readers loved *Old Christmas*. Caldecott's illustrations varied in size from full-page images to smaller sizes incorporated into the text.

They brought Irving's text to life in a style that was Caldecott's. The artist's drawings were not the caricatures he had often created for *London Society* and newspapers. Instead, he focused on illustrating the story to bring it to life.

Old Christmas was so popular that it was reprinted two months later. A reviewer wrote of *Old Christmas*:

> *The book is intended for the fireside of the reading folks in all classes. . . . so pleased are we with the designs, which exceed a hundred in number, that we have transferred them to our pages.*[2]

More Success

While busy working on his project with Cooper, Caldecott had begun illustrating for a new periodical. *Pictorial World* was started on March 7, 1874. The illustrated newspaper's art editor was Henry Blackburn. He could always rely on Caldecott for good work. Blackburn did not hesitate to ask the artist to contribute to the new publication. Caldecott was offered a position on the paper, but he did not accept

Caldecott's Studio

Randolph Caldecott completed his illustrations for *Old Christmas*, as well as many other drawings, at Henry Blackburn's cottage at Buckinghamshire in the English countryside.

it. Instead, he would contribute as he had done previously.

In 1874, Caldecott illustrated *Some of Aesop's Fables with Modern Instances*, which was translated by Alfred Caldecott, Randolph's brother. Cooper, who engraved the book, had suggested updating the tales by depicting modern scenes. Caldecott did not believe the book would do well once published. He wrote to a friend at the time, "Do not expect much from this book. When I see proofs of it I wonder and regret that I did not approach the subject more seriously."[3]

In 1874, Caldecott devoted time in his schedule to sculpt. He had been studying modeling with French sculptor Jules Dalou. In November, Caldecott worked on a cat sculpture. He finished *Crouching Cat* in December. Caldecott later illustrated a cat preying on a rat for *The House That Jack Built*, based on the nursery rhyme. The cat in the drawing resembles his *Crouching Cat* sculpture.

In January 1875, Caldecott also did some work painting furniture. He painted storks on a wardrobe. He also worked on a design featuring storks that he would paint in March. The illustrator created a number of sketches and diagrams as well.

From the book The House That Jack Built, *Caldecott's drawing of the cat may have been based on his* Crouching Cat *sculpture.*

But the year was not all work. Caldecott also took a vacation. He spent time near Whitchurch. This gave him the opportunity to return to the English countryside he had always loved. In May 1875, Caldecott resumed his partnership with Cooper. Another book was on the horizon, but not before Caldecott experienced an exciting first in London.

ROYAL ACADEMY EXHIBITION

Just as he had done in Manchester, Caldecott displayed his painting in London. In 1876, he had his first exhibit in London's Royal Academy. *There were Three Ravens sat on a Tree* received a wonderful reception. Members of the academy encouraged Caldecott to focus his time and energy on painting. Caldecott's sculpture, *A Horse Fair in Brittany,* was also displayed that year. It was highlighted in the *Saturday Review* on June 10: "Here a simply and almost rude incident in nature has been brought within the laws and symmetry of art."[4]

Caldecott was as busy as ever. He was creating a variety of work in multiple mediums, including illustration. The success of *Old Christmas* had prompted a sequel.

BRACEBRIDGE HALL

In 1877, Macmillan published *Bracebridge Hall*. The book was Caldecott and Cooper's follow-up to *Old Christmas*. The material for this second title came from Washington Irving's *Sketch Book*. *Bracebridge Hall* contained 116 illustrations. The second book was not as popular as its predecessor, but it sold enough copies to require a reprint later that year.

The Irving books introduced Caldecott to new readers and brought him acclaim and approval. They also further focused his attention on work. He wrote to a friend that he now had "a workshop, and I sometimes wish that I was a workman. Art is long: life isn't."[5] He continued to concentrate on his craft as well, though not solely on illustration. The second printing of *Old Christmas* and first and second printings of *Bracebridge Hall* in 1877 brought Caldecott great success that year, but he faced old challenges as well.

A Letter to Cooper

James D. Cooper worked with Randolph Caldecott on multiple projects. In addition to *Old Christmas* and *Bracebridge Hall*, Cooper engraved some of Caldecott's magazine illustrations. After reviewing some of Cooper's engravings, Caldecott sent him feedback. In a letter dated August 15, 1877, Caldecott wrote:

Dear Sir,
I am much obliged for proofs, which don't require touching from me as far as I can see.
I like No. 27 as rendered by you, but if you will allow me to again refer to the subject, I think you are not always fortunate about the position of your name. In this, the effect of the boy's foot being partly sunk in the dust is lost by having the name so close. . . . There would have been no harm in putting the name at the bottom edge of the cut.
You may think me too particular about this. As for myself I would rather leave out my initials than have them to interfere with the drawing—and I often do so—and in these slight drawings every little tells.
Yours very truly,
R. Caldecott[6]

ANOTHER CHANGE

The 30-year-old artist continued to have health issues. In January 1877, he traveled to the French Riviera on vacation to improve his well-being. Ideally, the warmer climate and time away from busy London would help him feel better. Thomas Armstrong joined Caldecott on his trip. The two friends spent their days drawing and painting the scenery that surrounded them.

Caldecott's time in France proved productive. He created more than 300 sketches. They were made into more than 50 illustrations that were published in the London newspaper *Graphic* in March and April of 1877. Caldecott continued to grow and achieve as an artist, but a new opportunity was in store for the young man. That same year, another man was experiencing changes with his work that would soon affect Caldecott and the world. ⌐

Caldecott's illustration, Bathing at Trouville, *was inspired by a trip to the Riviera.*

Caldecott's illustration of a farmer sowing seeds from
The House That Jack Built, *published in 1878*

Two Partnerships

Randolph Caldecott's partnership with James
D. Cooper in the mid-1870s was productive and
noteworthy. Caldecott's decision to work with
the engraver brought the artist new successes with
the books *Old Christmas* and *Bracebridge Hall*. He was

developing a style that a second teaming would make famous. Edmund Evans was England's most talented and successful engraver and color printer. His work with Caldecott would make the artist a beloved favorite in England and beyond.

EDMUND EVANS

Evans was planning to work on a book for Christmas with Walter Crane, an artist who illustrated children's books. When Crane decided not to work with Evans on the venture, the engraver sought out Caldecott for a partnership. Evans commissioned Caldecott for two books. He hoped the artist's reputation from *Old Christmas* and *Bracebridge Hall* would bring success to the new endeavor. This pairing would change the face of children's books.

The men made an uncommon business agreement. Rather than be paid after submitting his work to Evans, Caldecott agreed that he would accept payment only if the books sold. That meant that if the books did not sell, Caldecott would not make any money, even though he had done work on the project.

Evans described his agreement with Caldecott:

I agreed to run all the risk of engraving the key blocks which he drew on wood; after he had coloured a proof I would furnish him, on drawing paper, I would engrave the blocks to be printed in as few colours as necessary. This was settled, the key block in dark brown, then a flesh tint for the faces, hands, and wherever it would bring the other colours as nearly as possible to his painted copy, a red, a blue, a yellow, and a grey (I was to supply paper and print 10,000 copies, which George Routledge & Sons have published for me). [1]

Engraving

Edmund Evans was born in Southwark, London, in 1826. As an adolescent in 1840, Evans became an apprentice wood engraver to Ebenezer Landells. Later, he would become a successful color engraver.

In printmaking, images are put onto paper using ink. Wood engraving has been used primarily for magazine and book illustrations. To print one of his illustrations, Caldecott drew the image on a woodblock. Evans would use a cutting tool, called a graver, to cut away the area of the design that would not have color. Hardwoods allow engravers to create great detail that cannot be achieved by softer woods. Specifically, Evans would have been able to vary the spacing between the lines he engraved. This would let him use tone to create high-quality images. Once a block was engraved, Evans carefully painted its surface. After the paint was applied, a single piece of paper would be placed on the block and printed.

When he commissioned Caldecott to illustrate picture books, Evans was already a successful engraver with his own business. His work with Caldecott during the 1870s and 1880s changed the look of children's books.

The two books Caldecott illustrated for Evans were published in 1878 by George Routledge and Sons. The books did very well—perhaps better than Caldecott and Evans had imagined. The initial printing of *The House That Jack Built* and *The Diverting History of John Gilpin* was 10,000 copies for each title. All copies were sold before the books could be reprinted.

SCULPTOR

While working with Evans on the picture books, Caldecott continued to model and sculpt. Thomas Armstrong advised Caldecott on artistic studies and encouraged him to practice modeling. Caldecott had been studying clay modeling with Jules Dalou. And Armstrong taught Caldecott wax modeling for bas-reliefs, sculptures that project slightly from their background.

As he had done with painting, Caldecott used his talent and skill in modeling for interior design projects. In 1879, he worked on the capitals, or column tops, in Arab Hall. The project was a commission for Sir Frederick Leighton for work at his home, Leighton House, in Kensington.

Caldecott's illustration of the dog that worried the cat from
The House That Jack Built

Marian Harriet Brind

As Caldecott acquired new professional triumphs,
he experienced changes in his personal life as well.
The combination of his lifelong poor health and

hours of hard work made Caldecott realize that he needed to take better care of himself.

Now in his early thirties, Caldecott decided to leave London in 1879 for the countryside he so loved. He took up residence at Wybournes, a cottage in the small village of Kemsing, Kent. Ideally, his plan would lead to a more leisurely life. He could spend more time drawing nature and wildlife, just as he had enjoyed doing as a boy in Chester. On October 13, 1879, he wrote to a friend:

> *I am just now obliged to decline invitations to go and be merry with friends at a distance, because I am now living in this quiet, out-of-the-way village in order to make some studies of animals . . . which I wish to use for the works that I shall be busy with during the coming winter.* [2]

After moving to his new residence, Caldecott met Marian Harriet Brind. She lived approximately seven miles (11 km) from Wybournes in the town of Chelsfield. Caldecott and Brind became engaged shortly after they met. On January 17, 1880, Caldecott wrote to a friend who had sent good wishes about the engagement:

> *I am very pleased at receiving your congratulatory note. News will travel and I expected that you would hear of my*

schemes for happiness. Thank you all for sending good wishes for our future life.[3]

Caldecott's Wedding

Marian Brind lived with her family next to the Church of St. Martin-of-Tours, where she and Randolph Caldecott were married. She walked to her wedding. Randolph's brother, Reverend Alfred Caldecott, assisted in the ceremony.

The couple married on March 18, 1880, at the Church of St. Martin-of-Tours in Chelsfield. Marian then moved to Wybournes. Caldecott's life was going well: he had a wife, a home in the country, and a productive and successful career. Caldecott's collaboration with Edmund Evans would continue into the 1880s and bring the illustrator great accolades.

Caldecott's illustration of the man all tattered and torn from The House That Jack Built

One of Caldecott's illustrations from The Babes in the Wood

THE PICTURE BOOKS

Readers loved *The House That Jack Built* and *The Diverting History of John Gilpin*. Following the tremendous reception of the books in 1878, Caldecott and Evans worked on two more titles: *Elegy on the Death of a Mad Dog* and *The Babes in the Wood*.

A New Kind of Picture Book

The picture books were different from previous children's books. Their design and illustrations were unlike any seen before, including those of Caldecott's chief competitors, Walter Crane and Kate Greenaway. For example, illustrations did not always fill an entire page. Just as Caldecott had done in *Old Christmas* and *Bracebridge Hall*, some were small sketches mixed in with the text. A reviewer in the United States wrote in the New York newspaper the *Nation* in December 1878:

> *Mr. R. Caldecott's latest caricatures should not be overlooked by [suppliers] for the nursery. His* John Gilpin *and* The House That Jack Built *are . . . irresistibly funny as well as clever. One hardly knows which to admire most—the full page color-prints, or the outline sketches in the brown ink of the text. Happy the generation that*

Competition

Walter Crane began his career as a book illustrator before Caldecott. While the men competed in the same market, they were friends. Thomas Armstrong introduced them in 1877. They were about the same age. Both of their families came from Chester, and Crane knew Whitchurch, as members of his extended family lived there.

Kate Greenaway and Caldecott began illustrating children's books in England at the same time. Both worked with engraver Edmund Evans. They were competitors, but not enemies. They visited one another and exchanged letters, often discussing work issues. In a letter dated September 30, 1878, Caldecott wrote to Greenaway, "The brown ink . . . will not, when thickly used with a pen, keep itself entirely together under the overwhelming influence of a brush with water colour. I have found this out today."[1]

is brought up on such masters as Mr. Caldecott and Mr. Walter Crane.[2]

Caldecott's books lacked the ornate details and artistry often seen in Crane's illustrations and the simplicity and quaintness of Greenaway's style. Instead, he developed his own approach.

More than 100 hundred years later, Maurice Sendak, the illustrator and author of *Where the Wild Things Are,* described Caldecott's novel manner of drawing:

> *I can't think of the work of Caldecott without thinking also of music and dance. No one in a Caldecott book ever stands still. If the characters are not dancing, they are itching to dance. They never walk; they skip.*[3]

ONGOING PROJECT

Caldecott and Evans did not stop at four picture books. Caldecott drew dozens of illustrations for the picture books he created with Edmund Evans. In addition to creating the illustrations for the pages of the books, Caldecott also designed the book covers.

The artist and the engraver continued their partnership for several years and created 14 additional books:

"A Goose Girl" by Walter Crane

❖ *Sing a Song for Sixpence* and *Three Jovial Huntsmen* (1880)

❖ *The Farmer's Boy* and *The Queen of Hearts* (1881)

❖ *The Milkmaid, Hey Diddle Diddle,* and *Baby Bunting* (1882)

❖ *A Frog He Would A-wooing Go* and *The Fox Jumps over the Parson's Gate* (1883)

❖ *Come Lasses and Lads, Ride a Cock Horse to Banbury Cross,* and *A Farmer went Trotting upon his Grey Mare* (1884)

❖ *An Elegy on the Glory of Her Sex, Mrs. Mary Blaize* and *The Great Panjandrum Himself* (1885)

Caldecott chose the rhymes and the stories. In addition, the artist incorporated familiar objects from his life into his drawings. The tower of Whitchurch Parish Church appears in *The Great Panjandrum Himself*. Caldecott also included people he knew in his illustrations. In *The Babes in the Wood*, he drew Edmund Evans as one of the "ruffians strong" who was paid to kill the babes. As for his nonhuman characters, Caldecott often depicted animals wearing clothes and gave them human actions, such as dancing or walking down the street carrying a basket.

Caldecott's artistry breathed life into the picture books. He gave familiar nursery rhymes a new and special appeal. He did more than decorate the pages of the picture books; he interpreted the stories. In *Hey Diddle Diddle*, Caldecott's final illustration takes the story beyond what is written in the rhyme. After reading the words, "And the dish ran away with the spoon," the reader finds an additional illustration on the back of the page. This final image depicts what happened to the dish and the spoon after they ran away together. A knife and a fork (the spoon's parents), take the spoon from the dish. The fork (the spoon's father) has killed the dish. It is shattered on the floor and surrounded by other upset plates. The spoon's head hangs in sadness and shame as her parents lead her away.

In her 1946 book *Randolph Caldecott: An Appreciation*, Mary Gould Davis wrote of the artist's work:

> *When the children look at Randolph Caldecott's picture books they turn the pages very slowly. Each page tells a story, first in the action, then in the characters and, finally, in the little details that children love to linger over.*[4]

More Change

As Caldecott took on the role of children's book illustrator, he also experienced transitions in his personal life.

Evans on Printing

Edmund Evans was a talented and popular engraver and color printer during the Victorian era. He was particularly skilled at reproducing artists' works. He engraved the work of the successful British children's book illustrators of the time, including Walter Crane and Kate Greenaway, Caldecott's competitors. Evans described the printing process that required engraving a woodblock for each color used in the illustration:

> *The popular artists of the day were asked to supply drawings which were engraved on wood . . . one for a Red printing, the other for a Blue printing, the Red being engraved . . . to get the lighter tints such as faces, hands, etc.—the Blue block being engraved to get the best result of texture, patterns or sky, crossing the blue over the red to get good effects of light and shade. . . . the very most was made of each block by engraving so as to get the best result for the money!*[5]

After they were married in 1880, Randolph and Marian Caldecott lived at Wybournes for two years. They also traveled around England and spent time in Florence, Italy. In 1882, the couple moved to Broomfield, a house in Frensham, Surrey.

In addition to occupying the country house, Caldecott bought a house in Kensington. There, he built a studio. It was in the garden so that Caldecott could look out the window and take in the view.

Caldecott commuted to London to continue his work with Evans. Readers could not get enough of the books. But after illustrating 16 imaginative picture books for the engraver, Caldecott felt differently. By 1884, the 37-year-old was once again ready for change. Caldecott's next adventure would take him far from home.

Little Bo-peep has lost her sheep,
And can't tell where to find them;
Leave them alone, and they'll come home,
And bring their tails behind them.

This illustration of Little Bo-peep shows Kate Greenaway's simplistic style.

Caldecott's 1880 illustration from Sing a Song of Six Pence

GONE TOO SOON

Caldecott's decision to create picture books with engraver Evans changed the artist's life. Readers readily purchased the memorable titles that delighted young and old alike. By 1884, sales of the first 12 books surpassed

850,000 copies. In addition, the popular books received critical and public acclaim and made Caldecott known internationally.

ENOUGH

But by 1884, Caldecott did not welcome the books as readers did. He had grown tired of working on them and wanted to pursue other endeavors. On March 5, he wrote to Evans about his wish to end the project:

> *I do not want to do any more of this kind: but I shall be glad to hear if you & Routledge have a strong opinion that a couple more should be done. . . . I wish to turn my attention to something else. I have an idea of another single book . . . America is the place to publish more expensive books in.*[1]

Caldecott illustrated the final two picture books in the series following his letter to Evans. As he neared the end of his work on the project, Caldecott also illustrated three books for Juliana Horatia Ewing, a children's author. *Daddy Darwin's Dovecot* was published in 1884. *Jackanapes*, originally a magazine, was

"The Genius of Randolph Caldecott will stand for all time. Caldecott is lord of the nursery. No one ever yet approached him. He is supreme. Every nursery—every child's bookshelf that does not contain his Picture Books is poor indeed."[2]

—*Book jacket*,
R. Caldecott's Picture Book No. 4, *circa 1906*

made into a book in 1884, and *Lob Lie-by-the-Fire* was published in 1885.

However, these books did not compare to the picture books Caldecott created with Evans. Some of the illustrations were reprinted in *Aunt Judy's Magazine*, a publication for children. Art critic Gleeson White wrote of the illustrations, "Neither in the drawings nor in their engraving do you find anything else which is above the average of its class."[3] Caldecott wanted to stop illustrating picture books and focus on other projects. The work in these last few titles reflected his desire to move on.

A Trip Abroad

Caldecott had many friends, including artists and writers abroad. Fredrick Locker-Lampson, an English poet living in the United States, was one such friend. Locker-Lampson mentioned that Randolph and his wife, Marian, might enjoy a visit to the United States. Locker-Lampson and his wife, Jane, wanted to share their adopted country with the Caldecotts. The poet also thought the climate in the southern United States would be good for Caldecott.

In October 1885, the Caldecotts set sail from England to the United States. They had decided to go on a sketching trip around the country. The *Graphic* had commissioned Caldecott to record his observations and experiences on the trip. After landing in New York, the couple planned to visit Philadelphia, Pennsylvania. Next, they would head down the coast to the southern United States. There, the Caldecotts would stay for the winter, enjoying the warmer temperatures and gentler climates of Florida and Louisiana. The couple also planned to journey to California and Colorado. Finally, they would circle back to the East, where the travelers would complete their long U.S. tour in Boston, Massachusetts.

Letter to Locker-Lampson

After Frederick and Jane Locker-Lampson suggested the Caldecotts visit the United States, Randolph sent a letter to Frederick. Caldecott noted his plans for sailing to the United States and traveling around the country:

24 Holland Street, Kensington, W
18 October 1885

My dear Locker,
It was the suggestion of you and Mrs. Locker—you will remember—that we should go to America. We shall sail by Cunard ship Aurania *on 31st.*
I propose to take an easy tour—be guided by circumstances, of which the climate may be the chief. It may be pleasant to go quietly down the Eastern States to Florida and eventually on through New Orleans to South California, then up to North California and through Colorado and home by Boston?
I will give you news from some of the places.
Yours very truly,
Randolph Caldecott[4]

When he left England for his trip abroad, Caldecott was ailing. Recent years had been more difficult for the artist. The journey by ship to the United States proved challenging but not impossible. Caldecott did not get seasick, but his journey across the Atlantic was not a restful one. Still, as was always the case, Caldecott remained good-natured.

Upon arriving in New York, the couple had a short stay in the city before moving on to Philadelphia. Caldecott described the city:

> *At Philadelphia I was shocked by the lavish display of shop-signs and other street advertisements, and bewildered by the cobweb of telegraph wires and the forests of poles in the chief streets. There are some very clean streets of comfortable looking red houses with white doors, white or grey-green shutters, and well-kept steps; but the tram cars . . . and horse-railways run along these streets as*

Final Drawing

Caldecott set out for the United States with a plan to sketch the country. He actually started drawing during the journey across the Atlantic Ocean. *A Big Steamer Like This Never Rolls* shows passengers being tossed about the ship's deck.

Once on land, he sketched scenes from the various cities he visited. In South Carolina, Caldecott sketched *Negroes Loading Cotton Bales in Charleston*. It was his last drawing.

well as along the business thoroughfares, and produce an effect of incongruity and a lack of repose.[5]

After departing Philadelphia, the English couple proceeded, as planned, down the coast. The Caldecotts stopped in Washington DC. Randolph wrote of the city, "Washington, which used to be called 'The City of Magnificent Distances,' is now a fine town with imposing public buildings, and wide, clean streets."[6] After visiting the nation's capital, the Caldecotts visited Charleston, South Carolina. They reached St. Augustine, Florida, in December 1885.

A month later, on January 15, 1886, Marian Caldecott wrote to Jane Locker-Lampson. She explained that Randolph had been extremely sick in December and that he was getting better. However, Caldecott did not recover from his illness. He never traveled beyond Florida. Randolph Caldecott died on February 13, 1886, while in St. Augustine. He was 39 years old. His death certificate stated:

This certifies that Mr. Randolph Caldecott age 39, Born in Chester Engd. died at St. Augustine, Fla. February 13, 1886, of organic disease of the heart.

H. Caruthers

Physician[7]

Numerous Art Pieces

Randolph Caldecott left behind dozens of art pieces at his home when he died. These included 41 pictures and oil paintings and 12 sculptures that were made of bronze, plaster, and wax.

In her will, Marian Caldecott bequeathed her husband's artwork: "The picture of *A shepherd and sheep* at Cap Martin, Mentone, painted by my late husband which was given to me by Mr. Horace Mann, to the Rev. Alfred Caldecott of Great Oakley, Harwich.

"I bequeath all other pictures painted by him or which were written about him or his work to the Rev. Alfred Caldecott."[8]

Caldecott's body was not returned to England. Marian Caldecott had her husband buried in the Evergreen Cemetery in St. Augustine. Friends and admirers were shocked and saddened by Caldecott's unexpected death. The world had lost a kind and gentle man who was a talented artist. But Caldecott would not be forgotten. His gift and work would be enjoyed and honored long after the artist's untimely death.

Caldecott's 1881 illustration of the Queen of Hearts

Author and illustrator Maurice Sendak was the 1964 winner of the Caldecott Award for Where the Wild Things Are.

REMEMBERING
CALDECOTT

hroughout his life, Randolph Caldecott impressed people. His gentle nature and good humor endeared him to those he met. His love of and desire to study art were appreciated by other artists. From his newspaper sketches to his picture book drawings, Caldecott's talent as an illustrator informed and entertained readers young and old. The artist expressed himself in mediums that were not as well known to the general public, but they were appreciated by those who saw them.

REMEMBERING CALDECOTT

Caldecott's friends honored him with a memorial. Sir Alfred Gilbert designed a statue of a life-size child holding an image of Caldecott. The memorial, which is located in St. Paul's Cathedral in London, reads, "An artist whose sweet and dainty grace has not been in its kind surpassed: whose humour was as quaint as it was inexhaustible."[1]

There were written tributes as well. The following is a portion of a poem published in the *Graphic*:

Thy pencil drew, with loving, faithful care,
Each phase of human nature in its turn.
So that one looked and laughed, but yet would learn
To love all men the more for what was there.
Old folks would smile, and seem to see once more
The men and manners of a day gone by,
Whilst infants o'er thy "Picture Books" would pore,
And feast on Dreamland scenes with wondering eye.[2]

In 1890, editor, writer, and friend Henry Blackburn wrote a biography of Randolph Caldecott. The final chapter of the book states:

> *It can be said with truth that Caldecott was "a man of whom all spoke well." . . . No wonder—for was he not the very embodiment of sweetness, simple-mindedness, generosity, and honour?[3]*

Caldecott died a month before his fortieth birthday. His life was short. His career as an artist was considerably shorter. But neither Caldecott nor his work would be forgotten. Decades later, a publisher would honor the Victorian illustrator of children's books.

The Caldecott Medal

Frederic Gershom Melcher was a bookseller, an editor, and a publisher. Born and raised near Boston, Massachusetts, Melcher joined the publishing world while in his mid-teens. He later worked in Indiana before becoming an editor of the magazine *Publishers Weekly* in New York City.

Melcher had a keen interest in children's books. In 1919, he sponsored Children's Book Week, a celebration of children's books by booksellers, librarians, and schools. In 1921, Melcher created the Newbery Medal, an annual prize awarded to the author believed to have written the most notable children's book in the United States during the previous year.

In 1936, Melcher created a new award. He had learned of Randolph Caldecott and seen the artist's imaginative illustrations. Melcher said of naming the award after Caldecott:

> [his work] was very definitely the kind of thing where the

Caldecott Medal

The American Library Association considers Randolph Caldecott's original illustrations for children to be "unique to their time in both their humor, and ability to create a sense of movement, vitality, and action that complemented the stories."[4]

Named in his honor, the Caldecott Medal is considered to be the highest recognition an artist can receive for creating illustrations in a children's book that is published in English in the United States. Illustrators who have been awarded the Caldecott Medal include:

- *The Hello, Goodbye Window*
  Chris Raschka
- *Jumanji*
  Chris Van Allsburg
- *Madeline's Rescue*
  Ludwig Bemelmans
- *Make Way for Ducklings*
  Robert McCloskey
- *Officer Buckle and Gloria*
  Peggy Rathmann
- *Owl Moon*
  John Schoenherr
- *The Polar Express*
  Chris Van Allsburg
- *The Snowy Day*
  Ezra Jack Keats
- *Sylvester and the Magic Pebble*
  William Steig

interest was in the pictures, yet there never was a book where the text was inconsequential. It would be my impulse to say that we should include in the wording of the final statement that we suggest that the books be judged by the pictures but that the text should be worthy of the pictures.[5]

The editor and publisher wanted to establish an award for children's book illustrators similar to the Newbery Medal. Melcher ordered the full set of Caldecott's picture books for René Paul Chambellan, the sculptor given the task of designing the Caldecott Medal. The award was designed in 1937. Made of bronze, it features an illustration from *The Diverting History of John Gilpin.* It depicts Gilpin galloping away on a horse, disrupting the people and animals around him. Funny and alive with action, the image represents the style that was unique to Caldecott. The medal is also inscribed with the words "Awarded annually by the Children's and School Librarians Sections of the American Library Association."[6] In addition, the winner's name and the

The Caldecott Medal

The American Library Association has set the following guideline for awarding the Caldecott Medal: "The Medal shall be awarded annually to the artist of the most distinguished American picture book for children published in English in the United States during the preceding year. There are no limitations as to the character of the picture book except that the illustrations be original work. Honor Books may be named. These shall be books that are also truly distinguished."[7]

date are engraved on the back of the medal.

The first annual Caldecott Medal was awarded in 1938. The recipient was Dorothy P. Lathrop for her illustration of *Animals of the Bible*.

The Caldecott Medal has been awarded yearly since it was bestowed upon Lathrop in 1938. A committee determines the winner based on several criteria. One criterion is that the book must show "respect for children's understandings, abilities, and appreciations."[8]

In 1964, Maurice Sendak received the honored prize for *Where the Wild Things Are*, a book he illustrated and wrote. In *Caldecott & Co.: Notes on Books & Pictures*, Sendak addressed the work of Caldecott and other children's book illustrators. He wrote of Caldecott:

> *Caldecott's work heralds the beginning of the modern picture book. He devised an ingenious [combination] of picture and word, a counterpoint that never happened before. . . .*

Randolph Caldecott Society of America

The Randolph Caldecott Society of America "brings together those people who are dedicated to the remembrance, appreciation and promotion of . . . Randolph Caldecott (1846–1886) and his art."[9] The organization does this by producing and sharing information about Caldecott. It also maintains flowers on Caldecott's grave in Florida. Each year, the society donates that year's winner and honor books to the Randolph Caldecott Children's Room in the main branch of the St. Augustine, Florida, public library.

"A great nation is a reading nation."[11]
—Frederic Melcher

*Caldecott is an illustrator, he is a
songwriter, he is a choreographer, he is
a stage manager, he is a decorator, he
is a theater person; he's superb, simply.*[10]

An Adept Observer

Caldecott had devoted his talent, skill, and heart
to artistic endeavors. He recorded nature, people,
places, and events in a variety of styles. From his
paintings and sculptures to his illustrations, the
gifted artist gives readers an abundance of material
to study, appreciate, and enjoy. Through imaginative
illustrations in his 16 picture books with Edmund
Evans, Caldecott brought old stories new life
and new readers. He developed a children's book
illustration style the world had never seen before
and has since aspired to. Caldecott illustrated,
choreographed, and decorated the paper. He was
simply superb. And he simply won readers' hearts—
during his lifetime and well beyond. ⌒

Randolph Caldecott (1846–1886)

TIMELINE

1846	1861	1861
Randolph Caldecott is born March 22 in Chester, England.	Caldecott moves to Whitchurch, England, and works as a clerk at Whitchurch & Ellesmere Bank.	On December 7, Caldecott's drawing of the fire that destroyed the Queen Railway Hotel is his first published work.

1872	1873	1875
Caldecott moves to London to pursue a career in art.	Caldecott's first commissioned book, *The Harz Mountains: A Tour in the Toy Country*, is published.	Caldecott's *Old Christmas* is published.

1867	1869	1870
Caldecott moves to Manchester, England, to work as a bank clerk.	Caldecott exhibits his first painting while living in Manchester.	Caldecott visits London in May to meet Thomas Armstrong. It is the beginning of a friendship and mentorship.

1876	1877	1878
Caldecott exhibits his first painting in London and is encouraged to pursue the medium.	Caldecott's *Bracebridge Hall* is published.	Caldecott and engraver Edmund Evans publish *The House That Jack Built* and *John Gilpin*.

TIMELINE

1879	1880	1880
Caldecott's *Elegy on a Mad Dog* and *The Babes in the Wood* are published.	Caldecott marries Marian Harriet Brind on March 18.	Caldecott's picture books *Sing a Song for Sixpence* and *Three Jovial Huntsmen* are published.

1884	1885	1885
Caldecott's picture books *Come Lasses and Lads, Ride a Cock Horse,* and *A Farmer went Trotting* are published.	Caldecott's picture books *The Great Panjandrum* and *Mrs. Mary Blaize* are published.	In October, the Caldecotts depart by ship for the United States.

1881

Caldecott's picture books *The Farmer's Boy* and *The Queen of Hearts* are published.

1882

Caldecott's picture books *The Milkmaid, Hey Diddle Diddle,* and *Baby Bunting* are published.

1883

Caldecott's picture books *A Frog He Would A-wooing Go* and *The Fox Jumps over the Parson's Gate* are published.

1886

Caldecott dies on February 13 in St. Augustine, Florida.

1938

The first Caldecott Medal is awarded.

Essential Facts

Date of Birth

March 22, 1846

Place of Birth

Caldecott family home in Chester, England

Date of Death

February 13, 1886

Place of Death

St. Augustine, Florida

Parents

John Caldecott and Mary Dinah Brookes

Education

- ❖ King's School in Chester, England
- ❖ Manchester School of Art in Manchester, England
- ❖ Slade School of Art in London, England

Marriage

Marian Harriet Brind on March 18, 1880

Children

None

CAREER HIGHLIGHTS

❖ Caldecott's work was first published in the *Illustrated London News* on December 7, 1861.

❖ In 1869, Caldecott exhibited his first painting, *At the Wrong End of the Wood*, at the Royal Manchester Institution.

❖ In February 1871, Caldecott's work was published in *London Society*.

❖ Caldecott's first piece for *Punch*, a humor magazine, was published on June 22, 1872.

❖ Four small sepia drawings by Caldecott were displayed in London's Egyptian Hall as part of the annual Black and White Exhibition in 1872.

❖ Caldecott received his first commission for *The Harz Mountains: A Tour in the Toy Country*. Published in 1873, it included 24 of his drawings.

❖ *Old Christmas* was published in 1875. Due to its success, it was reprinted two months later.

❖ In 1876, Caldecott's painting, *There were Three Ravens sat on a Tree*, was exhibited at the Royal Academy in London.

❖ Caldecott illustrated *The House That Jack Built* and *The Diverting History of John Gilpin*. Ten thousand copies of each book were published in 1878 in the first printing.

❖ Beginning in 1878, Caldecott worked on 16 picture books with engraver Edmund Evans.

RESIDENCES

In England: Chester, Whitchurch, Manchester, London, Kemsing

QUOTE

"Art is long: life isn't."—*Randolph Caldecott*

ADDITIONAL RESOURCES

SELECT BIBLIOGRAPHY

Davis, Mary Gould. *Randolph Caldecott: An Appreciation*. New York: J. B. Lippincott Company, 1946.

Engen, Rodney K. *Randolph Caldecott: Lord of the Nursery*. London: Oresko Books Ltd., 1976.

Reichert, Gwen P., and Allan C. Reichert. "Randolph Who? From Where? What Did He Do?" *Randolph Caldecott Society of America*. 19 Oct. 2002. 4 Jan. 2009 <http://www.rcsamerica.com/>.

FURTHER READING

Billington, Elizabeth T. *The Randolph Caldecott Treasury*. New York: Frederick Warne & Co., 1978.

Caldecott, Randolph. *Randolph Caldecott's Picture Books*. San Marino, CA: Huntington Library Press, 2007.

Hutchins, Michael, ed. *Yours Pictorially: Illustrated Letters of Randolph Caldecott*. London: Frederick Warne & Co., 1976.

WEB LINKS

To learn more about Randolph Caldecott, visit ABDO Publishing Company online at **www.abdopublishing.com**. Web sites about Randolph Caldecott are featured on our Book Links page. These links are routinely monitored and updated to provide the most current information available.

Places to Visit

Kerlan Collection
The Children's Literature Research Collections
113 Elmer L. Andersen Library, 222 Twenty-first Avenue South,
Minneapolis, Minnesota 55455
612-624-4576
http://special.lib.umn.edu/clrc/kerlan/index.php
The collection consists of more than 100,000 children's books.
The Kerlan Collection has original artwork and manuscripts
for more than 12,000 children's books, including drawings and
watercolors by Caldecott.

Randolph Caldecott Drawings
Houghton Library, Harvard Yard, Harvard University
Cambridge, MA 02138
617-495-2440
http://oasis.lib.harvard.edu/oasis/deliver/~hou00319
This extensive collection has more than 500 works by Caldecott.
Pieces range from sketches and drawings for magazines to designs
for paintings, illustrated letters, art for the picture books, and a
self-portrait.

Randolph Caldecott Papers
The de Grummond Children's Literature Collection
McCain Library and Archives, University of Southern Mississippi
Box 5148, Hattiesburg, MS 39406
601-266-4349
www.lib.usm.edu/~degrum/html/research/findaids/caldecot.htm
In addition to material for several books, the collection contains
correspondence, photographs, postcards, and a rubbing of
Caldecott's tombstone.

GLOSSARY

acclaim
    To be well received or praised.

accolade
    Recognition or approval.

ailing
    To be sick or unwell.

apprentice
    A person training to be in a profession, such as printing.

bas-relief
    A type of sculpture that projects slightly from the background.

caricature
    A drawing of someone or something that is done in a cartoonlike manner by exaggerating some characteristics of the subject.

commission
    Art created under contract for a specific recipient.

correspondence
    Communication by letter.

disposition
    One's personality or nature.

engrave
    To carve into, such as in wood with a sharp tool.

graver
    One of a variety of cutting tools used by engravers to transfer an illustration into a woodblock during the printing process.

mentor
> A person who guides or teaches another person.

novelette
> A story that is longer than a short story and shorter than a novel.

picture book
> A book comprised mostly of pictures; this type of book is usually created for very young readers.

prone
> Being likely or given to having something.

refectory
> The dining area of a church or a monastery.

rheumatic fever
> A disease suffered mostly by children and young people. It causes fever, joint swelling and pain, and swelling in the heart.

sepia
> Various shades of brown ink.

transition
> A change.

vocation
> A person's career or profession.

wardrobe
> A large storage chest for hanging up clothing.

SOURCE NOTES

Chapter 1. An Artist at Heart
1. David Thomson. *England in the Nineteenth Century, 1815–1914*. New York: Penguin, 1978. 33.
2. Rodney K. Engen. *Randolph Caldecott: Lord of the Nursery*. London: Oresko Books Ltd., 1976. 8.

Chapter 2. Young Randolph
1. Rodney K. Engen. *Randolph Caldecott: Lord of the Nursery*. London: Oresko Books Ltd., 1976. 7.
2. Elizabeth T. Billington. *The Randolph Caldecott Treasury*. New York: Frederick Warne & Co., 1978. 22.
3. Rodney K. Engen. *Randolph Caldecott: Lord of the Nursery*. London: Oresko Books Ltd., 1976. 7.

Chapter 3. Manchester
1. Rodney K. Engen. *Randolph Caldecott: Lord of the Nursery*. London: Oresko Books Ltd., 1976. 8.
2. Michael Hutchins, ed. *Yours Pictorially: Illustrated Letters of Randolph Caldecott*. London: Frederick Warne & Co., 1976. 50.
3. Rodney K. Engen. *Randolph Caldecott: Lord of the Nursery*. London: Oresko Books Ltd., 1976. 8.
4. Manchester Archives and Local Studies. "Records of the Union Club, Manchester." *The National Archives*. 2009. 15 Feb. 2009 <http://www.nationalarchives.gov.uk/a2a/records.aspx?cat=127-m17&cid=0#0>.
5. Henry Blackburn. *Randolph Caldecott: A Personal Memoir of his Early Art Career*, London: Sampson Low, Marson, Searle, & Rivington, 1890. 5.
6. Ibid. 9–10.
7. Ibid. 14.
8. Ibid. 22.

Chapter 4. London
1. Rodney K. Engen. *Randolph Caldecott: Lord of the Nursery*. London: Oresko Books Ltd., 1976. 9.
2. Ibid. 10.

3. Henry Blackburn. *Randolph Caldecott: A Personal Memoir of his Early Art Career*. London: Sampson Low, Marson, Searle, & Rivington, 1890. 16–17.
4. Ibid. 28.

Chapter 5. Success!
1. James Hogg and Florence Marryat, eds. *London Society*. Jan. 1867. *Google Book Search*. 18 Feb. 2009 <http://books.google.com/book s?id=EH0UAAAAYAAJ&dq=London+Society+magazine&print sec=frontcover&source=bl&ots=516AR0423_&sig=J402UNcd9 QlXUQ9MFXZFvZF0Xl0&hl=en&ei=veCRSZCsO0T8NMe5-PQL&sa=X&oi=book_result&resnum=1&ct=result#PPA1,M1>.
2. Michael Hutchins, ed. *Yours Pictorially: Illustrated Letters of Randolph Caldecott*. London: Frederick Warne & Co., 1976. 60.
3. Rodney K. Engen. *Randolph Caldecott: Lord of the Nursery*. London: Oresko Books Ltd., 1976. 11.
4. Ibid.

Chapter 6. A New Direction
1. Rodney K. Engen. *Randolph Caldecott: Lord of the Nursery*. London: Oresko Books Ltd., 1976. 12.
2. Ibid.
3. Henry Blackburn. *Randolph Caldecott: A Personal Memoir of his Early Art Career*. London: Sampson Low, Marson, Searle, & Rivington, 1890. 96.
4. Ibid. 136.
5. Ibid. 97.
6. Michael Hutchins, ed. *Yours Pictorially: Illustrated Letters of Randolph Caldecott*. London: Frederick Warne & Co., 1976. 53.

Chapter 7. Two Partnerships
1. Rodney K. Engen. *Randolph Caldecott: Lord of the Nursery*. London: Oresko Books Ltd., 1976. 18.

Source Notes Continued

2. Henry Blackburn. *Randolph Caldecott: A Personal Memoir of his Early Art Career*. London: Sampson Low, Marson, Searle, & Rivington, 1890. 198.
3. Michael Hutchins, ed. *Yours Pictorially: Illustrated Letters of Randolph Caldecott*. London: Frederick Warne & Co., 1976. 144–145.

Chapter 8. The Picture Books
1. Michael Hutchins, ed. *Yours Pictorially: Illustrated Letters of Randolph Caldecott*. London: Frederick Warne & Co., 1976. 190.
2. Elizabeth T. Billington. *The Randolph Caldecott Treasury*. New York: Frederick Warne & Co., 1978. 38.
3. Ibid. 12.
4. Mary Gould Davis. *Randolph Caldecott: An Appreciation*. New York: J. B. Lippincott Company, 1946. 7.
5. Rodney K. Engen. *Randolph Caldecott: Lord of the Nursery*. London: Oresko Books Ltd., 1976. 18.

Chapter 9. Gone Too Soon
1. Rodney K. Engen. *Randolph Caldecott: Lord of the Nursery*. London: Oresko Books Ltd., 1976. 19.
2. Ibid. 7.
3. Gleeson White. *English Illustration, "The Sixties": 1855–70*. London: A. Constable and Co., 1897. 86. *Google Book Search*. 2009. 17 Feb. 2009 <http://books.google.com/ books?id=SPIjAAAAMAAJ&pg=RA3-PA127&lpg=RA3-P A127&dq=gleeson+white+English+Illustration&source=b l&ots=agz6QlxQ1U&sig=jOibwOi6pog_p-TsRDMPEyfx_ fA&hl=en&ei=Sl-USerNJ5CCNcG7sfML&sa=X&oi=book_ result&resnum=7&ct=result#PRA3-PA86,M1>.
4. Michael Hutchins, ed. *Yours Pictorially: Illustrated Letters of Randolph Caldecott*. London: Frederick Warne & Co., 1976. 245.
5. Elizabeth T. Billington. *The Randolph Caldecott Treasury*. New York: Frederick Warne & Co., 1978. 101.
6. Ibid.
7. Ibid. 54.
8. Randolph Caldecott Society UK. "Marian's Will." *RandolphCaldecott.org.uk*. 2004. 17 Feb. 2009 <http://www .randolphcaldecott.org.uk/marians_will.htm>.

Chapter 10. Remembering Caldecott

1. Randolph Caldecott Society UK. "St. Paul's." *RandolphCaldecott. org.uk*. 2004. 17 Feb. 2009 <http://www.randolphcaldecott.org.uk/st_pauls.htm>.

2. Randolph Caldecott Society UK. "Tributes." *RandolphCaldecott.org. uk*. 2004. 17 Mar. 2009 <http://www.randolphcaldecott.org.uk/tributes.htm>.

3. Henry Blackburn. *Randolph Caldecott: A Personal Memoir of his Early Art Career*. London: Sampson Low, Marson, Searle, & Rivington, 1890. 203–204.

4. American Library Association. "The Randolph Caldecott Medal." *ALA.org*. 2009. 8 Apr. 2009 <http://www.ala.org/ala/mgrps/divs/alsc/awardsgrants/bookmedia/caldecottmedal/aboutcaldecott/aboutcaldecott.cfm>.

5. Irene Smith. *A History of the Newbery and Caldecott Medals*. New York: Viking, 1957. 64.

6. American Library Association. "The Randolph Caldecott Medal." *ALA.org*. 2008. 25 Feb. 2009 <http://www.ala.org/ala/mgrps/divs/alsc/awardsgrants/bookmedia/caldecottmedal/aboutcaldecott/aboutcaldecott.cfm>.

7. American Library Association. "Terms and Criteria: Randolph Caldecott Medal." *ALA.org*. 2008. 19 Feb. 2009 <http://www.ala.org/ala/mgrps/divs/alsc/awardsgrants/bookmedia/caldecottmedal/caldecottterms/caldecottterms.cfm>.

8. Ibid.

9. Allan C. Reichert. "Randolph Who? From Where? What Did He Do?" *Randolph Caldecott Society of America*. 19 Oct. 2002. 4 Jan. 2009 <http://www.rcsamerica.com/>.

10. Maurice Sendak. *Caldecott & Co.: Notes on Books & Pictures*. New York: Farrar, Straus, and Giroux, 1988. 24.

11. Children's Book Week. "History." *BookWeekOnline.com*. 17 Feb. 2009 <http://www.bookweekonline.com/>.

INDEX

ABOUT THE AUTHOR

Rebecca Rowell has a Master of Arts in Publishing and Writing from Emerson College. She has edited numerous nonfiction children's books, including several biographies. Born and raised in Minneapolis, Minnesota, she has lived in Arizona, Massachusetts, and Austria. She once again resides in Minneapolis. This is her first book.

PHOTO CREDITS